# Table of Contents

The Alternatives . . . . . . . . . . . . . . . . . . . . . . . . . . . . . . . . . . .1
Sue the Bastards . . . . . . . . . . . . . . . . . . . . . . . . . . . . . . . . . . .7
Strange But True . . . . . . . . . . . . . . . . . . . . . . . . . . . . . . . . . .11
The Escort . . . . . . . . . . . . . . . . . . . . . . . . . . . . . . . . . . . . . . .13
Being Fired is Seldom a Surprise . . . . . . . . . . . . . . . . . . . . . .15
What It Takes to Get Fired . . . . . . . . . . . . . . . . . . . . . . . . . . .19
The Résumé . . . . . . . . . . . . . . . . . . . . . . . . . . . . . . . . . . . .21
The Best Time to Be Fired . . . . . . . . . . . . . . . . . . . . . . . . . . .27
Creditors, Leeches, and Other Scum . . . . . . . . . . . . . . . . . . .29
Too Old to Start Over . . . . . . . . . . . . . . . . . . . . . . . . . . . . . .33

| | |
|---|---|
| The Straws | 35 |
| Contract Work | 39 |
| The Volunteer | 43 |
| The Consultant | 47 |
| The Telegram | 49 |
| Hobbies | 53 |
| Training | 57 |
| Sales Jobs | 61 |
| The Phonies | 65 |
| Becoming an Entrepreneur | 69 |
| Some Tips | 77 |
| Job Fairs | 79 |
| Cyberjobs | 83 |
| The Application | 85 |
| Face to Face | 89 |
| Wowee! Whoopee! | 95 |
| What Do I Do With This Book Now? | 97 |

Andy Kane

# YOU'RE FIRED!

## How to Turn a Pink Slip into a Golden Opportunity

Paladin Press • Boulder, Colorado

**Other books by Andy Kane:**
Care and Feeding Of Tenants
No Waiting!
   How to Get What You Want, When You Want It
Tenant's Revenge

*You're Fired!*
*How to Turn a Pink Slip into a Golden Opportunity*
by Andy Kane

Copyright © 2002 by Andy Kane

ISBN 1-58160-321-5
Printed in the United States of America

Published by Paladin Press, a division of
Paladin Enterprises, Inc.
Gunbarrel Tech Center
7077 Winchester Circle
Boulder, Colorado 80301 USA
+1.303.443.7250

Direct inquiries and/or orders to the above address.

PALADIN, PALADIN PRESS, and the "horse head" design are trademarks belonging to Paladin Enterprises and registered in United States Patent and Trademark Office.

All rights reserved. Except for use in a review, no portion of this book may be reproduced in any form without the express written permission of the publisher.

Neither the author nor the publisher assumes any responsibility for the use or misuse of information contained in this book.

Illustrations by Steve Soeffing

Visit our Web site at www.paladin-press.com

# Preface

Why a book on being fired? Willie Sutton, the historic bank robber, when asked why he robbed banks replied, "That's where the money is." Being fired is a traumatic experience. It affects not just you, but your entire family, your creditors, your lifestyle, your health, everything! Why a book on being fired? Because it's needed!

Years ago, I found out that I had a limited talent for putting a pen to the paper. About the same time, I also discovered that I had a similar talent for getting fired!

When I was a young whippersnapper, I made another discovery. My mother was a widow of limited means (*very* limited) and I noticed that there was a direct correlation between how much money we had and what was on the dinner table. I discovered that if I worked a bit and gave the bucks to mom, we could go from tuna casserole to hot dogs!

## You're Fired!

I began delivering the evening paper and I collected, in that day, about 25 cents per customer per week. It was Monday through Saturday, no Sunday edition. I had a hundred customers, so for an hour or two after school, I could pick up $25 per week. After I paid the district manager for my papers, I could net about $7 per week or about $1.16 per afternoon.

After about six months, I was delayed by transportation from my school several times. My loyal, friendly neighbors, who were also my customers, called the paper and complained that I was "late." Big deal, so I got there at 5 P.M. instead of 3:30. Did the paper disintegrate in that extra hour? Was it unreadable? No, it was just as good, but a little late. Their complaints got me canned.

I was too young to retire, I did not have a fortune in the bank, and I could not collect unemployment insurance. What was I to do? I sat down and analyzed my qualifications. I was young enough to start over (12 years old) but what could I do? All my experience was in delivering newspapers. My résumé would be short. I hit upon a solution. I would apply to the morning paper as a carrier! I was accepted (possibly due to my experience or the fact that the carrier in my area just quit) and began my new job.

Why am I telling you this ridiculous story? To demonstrate one important thing. Being fired is good 99 percent of the time. My new route had 125 customers. It was seven days a week because it had a Sunday edition. It paid 35 cents per week per customer. After I paid the district manager for my papers, I netted 12 bucks a week! The firing had caused me to get a *better* job! More money! But that's not the end. I lived in the frigid north—not Alaska, but a city on the New York/Canadian border that has cold, snow, sleet, rain and, every once in awhile, a sprinkling of sun. My new route included about 55 units of apartments. I could deliver all the apartments by walking through the halls. Nice and warm! An added bonus after being fired!

## Preface

I have found by careful research that you almost always find a better job each time. I sort of looked forward to those magic words—you are fired!—at the end of each of my various careers.

Now why should you listen to my advice on what to do after you're fired? When I read a book, I always look at the author's credentials before I spend my valuable time plowing through 195 pages on how to become successful. If I find the author is in *Who's Who* and has a private jet and a summer home in Switzerland, I heed his advice and read on. If the author's address is that of a mission or soup kitchen and the book was self-published on a secondhand copier, I toss it and move on.

I would classify myself somewhere in between the tycoon and the bum. I have had a lot of jobs and have gotten fired from most because of my attitude or personality, but as I say,

*You're Fired!*

each time the next job was better! I have what today would be considered a limited education (Edison Tech High School, class of '54, lower half). I have written a book about jobs based upon my experience in the work place (*Jobs That Suck and Some That Don't*, Paladin Press). I presently operate four businesses: Andy Kane Realty Corp. (a real estate business), Allstate Rentals (an apartment and home rental agency), Hacienda Holding Corp. (a management company), and Unique Vacations USA (a travel advisory company). I also write a book or two in my spare time.

OK, that's enough background. Let's get to what you are going to do with the rest of your life, once you are again gainfully employed!

# The Alternatives

There are many alternatives to choose from when you get your pink slip and many people pick the wrong ones because they appear easiest. I will name a few:

1. Gas pipe (highly favored after the crash of '32)
2. Car running in your closed garage, your favorite station on the radio
3. A rope over the attic rafter and the other end replacing your neck tie
4. Swan dive off highest bridge or building
5. Retraining (almost as bad as 1 through 4!)
6. Networking (hounding your friends)
7. Relocating (grass always appears greener on the other side of the street!)

# You're Fired!

8. Head hunters (not a bad idea!)
9. Early retirement and a rocking chair
10. Entrepreneurship
11. The bottle

There are many others, but these are the usuals; the ones that pop into your head as you drag your broken body out to the parking lot with your walking papers in your pocket.

Let's consider the first four together, because they all result in the same conclusion—a long funeral procession and a visit to the pearly gates (I hope).

*Solutions 1—4.* Before you do any of these, consider this. How many good times have you had on this planet, so far? They will end. Do you have family, kids, dog or cat? This will wreak havoc with their lives, even if you have a massive insurance policy (check the limits for self-inflicted death). All your nice suits and ties will be on some vagrant after the little lady cleans out your closet and gives them to the Salvation Army. The dog will be sitting on the front steps for weeks waiting for you to come home so he can jump on you (the cat won't care), and your wife will have to get a facelift before she returns to the bar scene. Most important, you will never get revenge on the schmuck who canned you! Pulling your own plug is *never* a good alternative.

I have known many who did it and I was always annoyed that they did it. One friend was young and extremely handsome, a very intelligent guy. His name was Jim Becker. After he lost his job, he and his car went into a local river. He was saved and the paper indicated that he had "fallen asleep" at the wheel. Several days later, I drove by the spot where the paper indicated the "accident" had occurred. The tire tracks left the road at a 90-degree angle and between the road and the river, there was a tree. The tire tracks went *around* the tree! This lead me to believe that it was a suicide attempt.

I saw Jim when he was released from the hospital. I said, "If you ever do that again, let me know so I can sell tickets. Evel Knievel made a lot of money when he tried to jump the Snake River Canyon!" We were pretty good friends and his mother was my lawyer's secretary. I said this to Jim to break the ice and let him know I was his friend. His reply, and I can still hear his words today, was, "That's *one thing* I am not going to do again!" I mistakenly thought he was telling me that he was not going to try to take his life, again. Two weeks later, I realized my interpretation of this statement was wrong. Jim meant he was not going to try the river jump again, but he did something else. I was also his landlord and two state police investigators came to see me with the sad news that Jim had gone to the hereafter via a shotgun blast. To this day, I think what a life he could have had with his movie-star looks and brains. Suicide is never a good choice when some minor thing like unemployment hits your life.

*Solution 5: Retraining.* It can't hurt if you don't have anything lined up. Let's say you are a skilled machine operator and robots and cheap labor in China have made your job expendable. Many states, agencies, and schools offer training at reduced cost or free. Since you have some free time, you might as well put that time to good use. Don't spend this time training for another job in the same industry because you are again putting your future in the hands of the robots and cheap labor. Try paralegal, advertising, sales, or other interesting occupations. It's nice to have a back-up occupation. I was once an instrument maker and to this day I still have my toolbox and tools, just in case.

*Solution 6: Networking.* It's a fairly new word and it means bugging every single friend you have made since the third grade to get you an interview at the sweatshop where they work. Call everyone, including those who you hate and those who hate you. Just because someone hates you does not mean they won't help you get a job. The reason is that it may help them and everybody looks out for No. 1 (themselves). Their company may have been looking for a "Class A journeyman widget maker" for a year! He hates your guts, but by recommending you for this opening, he puts a feather in his cap. He's happy (with the feather) and you're happy (with the job). It happens and I have firsthand knowledge of it.

*Solution 7: Relocation.* There is only one reason to relocate and that is if you're joining the federal witness relocation program. People always think things will be different someplace else, but the loss of a job or a divorce is a product of your own personality and attitude. If you move to "East Podunk" your personality and attitude will go with you. Furthermore, all the contacts that you have made will stay at the old address and you will lose the benefit of these contacts. You will have to learn new everything (such as vendors, grocery store, local laws, pizza delivery, lawyers, doctors, and street patterns) in addition to looking for a job! It's not a good idea. One exception is if your occupation or trade was in demand at Xerox in Rochester, New York, and the same skill is in demand in Pasadena, California, for more bucks. If Pasadena will pay relocation and a bonus . . . relocate!

*Solution 8: Headhunters.* These placement experts sell bodies; that's how they make their living. Like you putting a computer together with pieces and parts from various suppliers, they match up what you do with what some company needs. These are specialists in the field and some just handle presidents of large corporations. You will never see the president of General Motors over at Ford in the employment office filling out an application. The corporate headhunters line these deals up. If you are unemployed, find a headhunter who specializes in your field and sign up with him.

*Solution 9: Early retirement.* If you have some bucks set aside, or a steady income from book royalties (ha,ha), patents, or other reliable sources, consider the rocking chair. I actually did retire several times, but became bored very soon. I have known many who did retire early and enjoyed it. Their theory was that they are not rich, but can survive. Their health is good now so they can do a lot that they may not be able to do if they wait until 65. It's hard to ride your Harley cross-country if you are on oxygen or need a seeing-eye dog for navigation. This decision is very individual and should be weighed carefully.

*Solution 10: Entrepreneurship.* I can give you names of hundreds of individuals who started some type of business after getting the ax at the mill. I think it's a great idea because that's actually what got me started. I had a pocket full of severance pay, my vested interest in my pension, and some bonuses to hold me over for a few months and that's all I needed.

There is a group of people who have left Xerox for various reasons—laid-off, fired, etc. This group has an organization called Xerox-X and for networking purposes, they publish a directory. There are 155 pages with the names, addresses, and titles of these ex-Xerox people. A good share of these people were dismissed by Xerox, which usually indicates that the company did not think they had much value. Surprise! If you flip through this directory of more than 1,800 people who were mostly drummed out of the big copier company, you will find that approximately one third are now presidents or CEOs of companies they joined or started themselves! There is not a page in this directory that does not contain at least two CEOs or presidents. It's like a *Who's Who* of entrepreneurship. (I'm on page 59!)

*Solution 11: The bottle.* This is only slightly better than 1 through 4! It actually can produce the same results depending on your liver or whether you drive or not. This is not just an out for lowlifes who are laid off. It is an option for lawyers and other professionals. My advice is one or two a day to loosen up, but I have seldom heard of headhunters or employers searching their neighborhood bars looking for someone to fill an important vacancy at the local manufacturers. Alcohol causes depression and that is something you probably don't need on top of your downsizing. Bars are for losers. Stay sober until you get back on the payroll at your new job and then tie one on!

# Sue the Bastards

I hate to even suggest this avenue. I am an employer and I have been sued. It's an inconvenience, especially when it is a false suit. I was once sued by a secretary that had worked for us for 12 weeks. She sued for $14 million.

When the discovery period of the suit began, we found out that I was the fourth employer she had sued, all after 12-14 weeks on the job. Why, then, had I never seen her name in the paper or on TV? All were local employers; a large national gas retailer, a national insurance company, and nationwide department stores. *Never* was there a word in the media. Later I found out that to avoid having their names dragged through the mud, these national companies quietly settled out of court.

## You're Fired!

There is a really good chance that if you sue because they fired you for being "bald" or "fat" or "ugly," they may have trampled on some local, federal, or state law that could be construed as discrimination. Rather than have the case on the 6 P.M. news, some companies write a check! Every area has attorneys who specialize in these types of cases. A large soda-pop bottler (who I won't mention by name, but their bottles have a distinctive shape) recently agreed to pay billions to settle with a group that claimed they were dismissed or failed to be promoted because of their race.

Did the company lie to you to get rid of you? A large film manufacturer (who I also won't name, but their film comes in a yellow box) offered a "buyout" (same as being fired, but nicer name) to certain employees. This buyout was good for a certain period of time and during this period, the employees were interviewed by the personnel department and an offer was made. Free teeth cleaning for five years, a book of carwashes, a Christmas turkey, and $5,000 in cash! Every employee asked, "Is that it? Will there be a better buyout in the future?" They were assured that it was *the* deal and they should grab it while they could. Hundreds took the deal. As soon as the deadline passed for taking this wonderful buyout, the company announced a new buyout plan—free teeth cleaning for five years, a book of carwashes, a Christmas turkey and *$35,000* cash! Another amazing thing happened. The employees in the personnel department who had called the first plan the cat's meow and "the best the company ever will have" suddenly began retiring under the new buyout plan. Obviously they were well aware that the first plan sucked and the new plan was coming shortly. *No* employees in the personal department left during the first buyout and many left during the second, so they were lying to the employees. The victims of the first buyout banded together (misery loves company) and hired an attorney to sue the company.

*Sue the Bastards*

Every situation is different but there are reams of laws governing what is permissible as a reason for canning you. Some questions that may or may not apply to you are:

- Are you gay and the boss is straight?
- Are you not gay and the boss is?
- Do you have unusual religious beliefs like sacrificing a chicken or doing voodoo during your morning break?
- Are you handicapped or pregnant?
- Are you a boy?
- Are you a girl?
- Are you obese?
- Are you a minority and company is non-minority owned?
- Are you not a minority and company is minority owned?
- Are you old, maybe just four days away from being fully vested in your pension?
- Are you driving a Dodge and working at a General Motors assembly plant?

*You're Fired!*

There are hundreds of laws regarding workplace firings and you should consult a lawyer that specializes in filing these types of claims. The law you want is the Title VII of the Civil Rights Act of 1964. The list above is not a complete list of things you can claim, but it should get your mind working. I don't suggest filing a frivolous suit, but if you see a possibility or pattern, you may have a case. I don't think you will get enough to retire on with a claim, and they usually take years to settle, but there is also the chance that you could strike it rich. Suing is the American way. You can even become president by suing. God bless America!

# Strange But True

We have talked about being fired. You got fired, everybody knows you were fired, your kids told their playmates that daddy got fired, your father-in-law called from Utah and said he heard you got fired. The word *fired* is burned into your brain.

Now, let's think back to the day you got fired. Did they say you were fired? Did any of the documents that they gave you have the word fired in them? Have you ever heard the boss tell someone they were fired? Amazing. The word *fired* is never heard, spoken, or written in the workplace. It's not politically correct to use this horrid word. This book probably won't sell just because of the title!

I believe that every company has a person whose job is to find other words, terms, or sayings to avoid using the word

## You're Fired!

fired. Everybody knows they are fired, have been fired, or are going to be fired, but the word is never spoken! I believe it's to soften the blow and reduce animosity. You will be:

- Temporarily laid off (Ask how long temporarily is.)
- Downsized (Will your clothes still fit now that you are downsized?)
- Surplus
- Dismissed
- Part of a reduction in plant personnel

But *never* fired. This word has disappeared with the likes of fireman (now firefighter), mailman (now postal worker), and other job descriptions that have been the target of political correctness.

My book is almost obsolete already because there is almost no chance you will ever be *fired*!

# The Escort

A friend of mine, who is about six-foot-ten, recently retired from the police department. He was immediately hired by a local corporation to assist with downsizing. His job was to lend muscle when some poor slob was terminated. As the boss was giving someone his walking papers, Tom would stand nearby. Many long-term employees develop "desk rage" when things get rough.

The thought of layoffs cause stress to build up and the trigger can be the walking-paper presentation. This is possibly the highest stress period of the employee's entire career and you never know what to expect. There have been many cases of someone returning with a firearm to settle the score with the company or its supervisors. Tom's looming presence usually convinces the dismissed employees that it's time to go quietly.

## You're Fired!

# Being Fired is Seldom a Surprise

Deep in your heart you knew you were going to get the boot. You probably knew it for some time. What did you do? Probably lit a candle at church, said an extra prayer (or sacrificed an extra chicken), and were on your best behavior on the job. That was all a waste of time and you got the ax (or will get it) anyway.

Once you get that gut feeling (and I'm a firm believer in gut feelings), you should immediately begin preparing for your next adventure. Is your résumé up to date? Do you have enough copies? Are there items that you have designed or built that could serve as a sample of your work (that fit in your lunch box!)? All these may help you land on your feet as you go out the door next week. Forget about any secrecy clause or agreements with this company because they don't

care about you. If you have just invented a process for turning cat urine into a new fuel, steal it. Photograph it. Memorize the formula and keep it safe. You may find another company interested and this could be your meal ticket for a year or two.

If you have been instrumental in creating some product that is in production, get all the brochures, photos, or spec sheets and keep them for examples of your fine work.

Since you might need a reference for a future job, find someone that will probably be staying at the company and make friends with them. Tell them that you don't trust the boss to give you a good reference and could they help? The next application you fill out, instead of listing "Mr. Big Wheel" as your boss, you list "Mr. Friend" and give his extension number. I would also give him a simple script for future use. For example: "Andy Kane did work here from September 5, 1998 to August 10, 2000. We don't usually give out addi-

*Being Fired is Seldom a Surprise*

tional information over the phone, but I can tell you personally, he was the best designer (sweeper, cook, etc.) that we ever had." Since whoever is calling had called the main number for the widget factory and dialed your friend's extension number, they probably will be satisfied that you did work there and you are the greatest designer (sweeper, cook, etc.) in the universe!

When you get the boot, they want you out pronto! Usually within five minutes. You will have an escort, probably a guy who looks like a retired champ from the World Wrestling Foundation. Plan ahead when you feel the day may be approaching. Take home any questionable items in advance. Keep only a minimum of items in your desk or files. Duplicate your computer files and keep them at home. Don't car pool or you may be hitchhiking home.

Whatever you do, leave with dignity. Don't swing at the bearer of the bad (actually good) news. Remember, if you get

violent, there is a six-foot-ten Tom somewhere nearby. This advice is the logical advice, but if you feel that a few quietly spoken words (f*#! you, you fat b@*%@*#) will make you feel better on the drive home, I understand!

# What It Takes to Get Fired

Of course, there are the obvious ways to get yourself fired, such as stealing large sums of money or having elicit sex on the job. Everyone I know who's gotten the ax immediately thought, "What did I do wrong?" If you have been terminated, I'm sure you had this same feeling. It's normal. Most likely, you did nothing wrong and your dismissal had more to do with when you were hired (seniority), what you did for the company (critical skills), or what the main product was (hula hoop manufacturer).

I have found one big thing that also helps the management pick your number. That's personality and attitude. If you are a meek little church-mouse type, follow all instructions and commands without hesitation regardless of how stupid they are, never cause waves or make suggestions of "better" ways to do things, you are probably safe because you "go with the flow." If you are outgoing or make any waves, you don't kiss the boss's rear end frequently, you allow outside interests to creep into your work space, and you look or dress differently than the rest of the employees, you can be sure your name will reach the top of the hit list.

If you fit in this last description, you probably know it. I did, and the last job that I had was approximately 25 years ago. Since I am still friends with many of the zombies who worked with me at that time, I get invited to various retirement parties for these people. I have yet to go to one of these where my name has not come up during the speeches—and I've been gone 25 years! They *still* talk about my offbeat antics after all this time! That certainly reinforces my opinion that if you are unusual and don't fit the mold, the powers that be will put you high on the list of people that should be shown the door.

Your contribution to the overall well being of the company is second to your personality and action in the workplace. You could be the No. 1 designer or engineer and your rear end is still on the line if your personality does not fit in with the group.

# The Résumé

It is said that every résumé that has been written is possibly 200 percent bull crap. Every interviewer knows that and will possibly discount at least 50 percent of what you claim as your résumé. There are many companies that specialize in writing résumés. Your PC probably has a boilerplate template that you can use, and these procedures work well most of the time. One thing that is very important is the old acronym, "KISS" (Keep it simple, stupid!).

If you are a janitor and empty wastebaskets all night, do not classify yourself as a "recycling engineer!" They may be looking for a janitor and pass you up because they think a "recycling engineer" is something else. Be honest because, as ridiculous as it may sound, honesty is the best policy when job hunting. I conned my way into several jobs with false claims and once I got those jobs, it was really hard to perform and took a toll on my mind. It doesn't hurt to flower up your résumé a little but draw the line at completely false claims (such as saying you were the president/CEO when you were just a billing clerk).

When you have a résumé prepared, be sure your photo appears in it. Looking nice—having good grooming and decent clothing and being clean cut—means a lot if the job involves dealing with the public. Do not print the copies on a Xerox copier using standard 20# bond copy paper; it will look cheap if you do. Spend some money and have it reproduced on quality paper. (Note: an exception to this rule is when you are applying to a conservation-minded group—Tree Huggers of America or Owl Savers International. If you apply to one of these groups, print the résumé on "recycled" paper.)

Be sure the references listed are favorable to you; have the correct phone numbers and extensions listed along with the correct mailing addresses. If someone is interested in your skills, contacting these references should be as easy as possible.

You should also post your résumé on any Web sites that cater to your qualifications and have references on your résumé to any Web site that you use. E-mail your résumé to prospective employers.

As I mentioned previously, photos of special products you were involved in can be included on your résumé and will make it more likely to be read. One size does not fit all. Tailor-make each résumé to fit the job description, making a few adjustments to create a new résumé for a particular job. Highlighting certain tasks and dropping others may be the difference between your résumé hitting the bull's eye instead of the trash basket!

If your talents are not suitable for composing your résumé, try a professional résumé service. Many will also offer distribution to employers. These companies are usually listed in your Yellow Pages.

## The Résumé

Some of the best methods of getting your résumé in front of a decision maker are as follows, listed in the best way first:

1) Hand carry it to the decision maker for the company you wish to join.
2) Ask someone at the company you know is a friend of the decision maker to take it to them. (Note: Be sure your friend is not a BS-artist. There are many who say, "Yeah, I have lunch with the president twice a week," when they actually just eat in the same company cafeteria.)
3) Bring the résumé into the human services offices in person.
4) Mail your résumé in those special cardboard-style envelopes available from office supply stores. They look like overnight or other important U.S. Post Office mailers, but they can be sent regular first-class mail. If the postage is $1.50, do not use the machine stick-on paper stamp issued by the post office. Use various stamps in the quan-

tity necessary to reach $1.50. It makes your envelope look even more important and increases your chance of having your résumé actually looked at.

5) Mail in first class, 9x10 Tyvek envelopes. This is the kind that has green triangles around the edges and is usually used to mail important documents like stock certificates. Whatever you do, do not, absolutely *do not* use #10 business envelopes or letter-size envelopes. You have put a lot of effort into creating your résumé, but the delivery task is just as important.
6) Have the headhunter or résumé factory send it out using the shotgun approach along with 75 other résumés, some of which may be better than yours.
7) Send it via e-mail.

## The Résumé

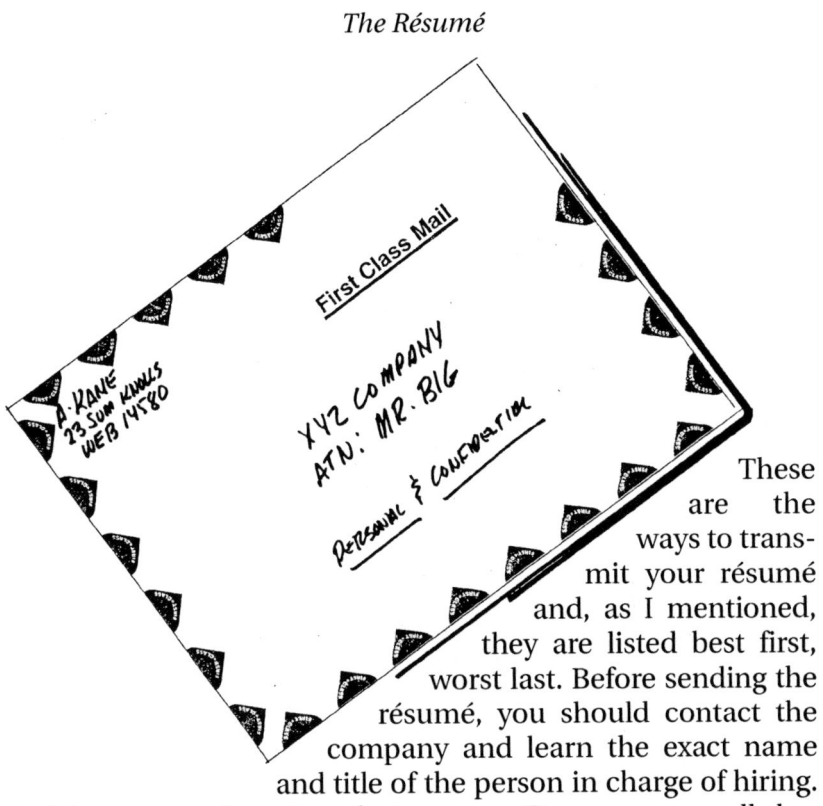

These are the ways to transmit your résumé and, as I mentioned, they are listed best first, worst last. Before sending the résumé, you should contact the company and learn the exact name and title of the person in charge of hiring. Address your résumé to that person. (Be sure you spell that person's name right so you don't offend him or her to start off!)

Many people send a floppy disc or CD/ROM with all their information on it, but I do not recommend this. The person who gets your résumé wants to see it the second it comes out of the envelope. A hard copy professionally prepared is best. For safety reasons, many companies will not stick a strange floppy disc in their computer for fear that a disgruntled ex-employee may send something with a virus in it to get revenge.

# The Best Time to Be Fired

I can only think of one time that being fired is not a traumatic, heart-stopping catastrophe. That would be the day after you win the Powerball lottery! Any other time is bad! When you get fired, you immediately think, "Why now? Just two weeks before Christmas (before Thanksgiving, before Easter, before Memorial Day, before the Fourth of July)?" Get the idea? Holidays are spaced throughout the year for one reason: so you can get fired "just before the holidays." Other factors that make being fired more traumatic are:

- Your wife is pregnant and going into labor just as you are leaving labor.
- You just bought a new car or house and the first payment is next week.

*You're Fired!*

- All your credit cards are maxed out.
- Your insurance will lapse next week if you don't pay the premium.
- Your income tax return needs a small check ($5,000) before you can send it in.
- The foreclosure letter says to contact their attorney next week with a payment or call the movers.
- The movers want money up front before they start packing.
- The rent just went up.
- All of your kids and pets need their shots.
- There was a margin call from your broker.
- All your investments are at an all-time low.
- Every employer in town has a "no help wanted" sign in his window.
- The bankruptcy attorney wants his fees up front.
- What else is troubling you, brother?

You may feel that being fired could not have come at a worse time, but as you can see above, there is never a good time to get the ax. Live with it and move on to a better life. Remember being fired is just a stepping-stone to a better job!

# Creditors, Leeches, and Other Scum

Here is when being creative comes in handy. The people you owe money to are still working. They still have a job to do—to hound the hell out of you to get your food money to keep themselves from being fired.

The first month or two won't be too bad. There will be letters and perhaps polite phone calls. The third month it gets a little rougher; they don't talk nice anymore and the letters become more threatening. They mention attorneys, judgements, court costs, and broken limbs. You have to answer with a disguised voice and say, "No, Nelson is not here. I'm his grandfather. Nelson is out of town until the 15th." The mail begins piling up, unopened. You draw the blinds and turn the lights off when you hear a knock at the door. But avoidance is not the best avenue to take.

*You're Fired!*

Again, being honest is still the best policy. Tell these creeps that you don't have a job, don't have any money, you are looking for a job (do they need any more phone harassers?), and that you would like to work something out. Ninety-nine percent will work with you. They don't really want your house or car. Their business is money. Your car or house cannot be banked. They would have to resell and they would lose money on the deal. They will do just about anything to get cash instead of property.

During this period of forced vacation, you should be especially careful to not have too much money in your bank account. Creditors may freeze your assets or have funds withdrawn. Keep the money in a safe place (such as a coffee can buried in the back yard) until creditors have been satisfied.

If your debts are overwhelming, a bankruptcy may be your best solution. Before undertaking this route, consider this: many potential employers run a credit report to deter-

## Creditors, Leeches, and Other Scum

mine how responsible you are, and if a bankruptcy is on that credit report, you could miss out on a job. Keeping that in mind, sometimes a bankruptcy may be the only way to clear up your debts.

I would not consider a bankruptcy filing for a small amount of debt (less than $50,000). One of the reasons is you must wait seven years before you can use bankruptcy again. If you use this system now and in a year or two something big happens (such as an illness, a judgement in the high figures, or an accident claim against you), you will not have bankruptcy to fall back on.

If you do decide on using bankruptcy to rid your life of the bloodsuckers, be sure you pick a good attorney. The Yellow Pages may give you a clue who to call. Keep in mind that a big ad does not necessarily mean the attorney is the best—it just means he spends the most for his ad. Instead, visit a bankruptcy court. They are in your nearest federal building. Listen to the attorneys who are practicing in that court and pick the one you like. You will be eligible for either a Chapter 13 (adjusted payback over a set period of time) or a Chapter 7 (creditors get crap, you walk away clean). Unless a foreclosure auction has already been scheduled for next week, filing bankruptcy is not urgent. I would not advise doing anything against the law, but I have heard of people using up whatever credit they had before filing. They ran every credit card to the limit. I actually had a tenant who had a gas credit card that had some free play left on it. Before his filing, he purchased assorted batteries, anti-freeze, and many, many tires. His apartment became the second largest auto-parts store in the area!

I'm not recommending this, just telling you what I have seen. Do not attempt to transfer property or vehicle to your girlfriend, because these items have a time limit and dates are easily available if someone wanted to get you for bankruptcy fraud. As soon as you file, all creditors must, by law, stop hounding you. When they call, simply say, "I have filed for bankruptcy protection. My attorney's name is John Belluscio and his phone number is 555-4635." That's it! (Unless you are actually using John Belluscio, put your own mouthpiece's name and phone number in the sentence.) Bankruptcy is a federal plan. God bless America!

# Too Old to Start Over

Remember I mentioned this problem when I was fired from my paper route at age 12? I decided that I was young enough to keep going. Possibly you are older than 12, maybe even in your 40s, 50s, or 60s and got the ax.

Can you start over?

I will sum this up with one example. Do you know where the colonel got the funds to start his fried chicken empire? From his very first Social Security check! It can be done!

## You're Fired!

# The Straws

Every person that has been canned has been tempted to grab at straws. Because of this, many companies have been set up to offer straws and grab your money.

You have seen the ads in the supermarket tabloids: "Stuff envelopes at home and make $500 a week, guaranteed!" This scheme works something like this: You send in $100 for "supplies" to start up. The company sends you envelopes to stuff and circulars to stuff in them. You send them to all the relatives and friends that you and the spouse have (using your own postage, of course). If one of these suckers sends for one of the amazing 10-cent items advertised in this circular and encloses $5.95 + $1.95 shipping and handling, you get a commission on that great sale!

Another straw you can grab is being a "rack jobber" for

four or five grand. No selling involved. For your investment, you receive a bunch of wire racks and a cheap product to put on the racks—such as greeting cards or novelties. You go out and get merchants, like the guy who runs the corner store, to let you put your rack in their store for a commission on sales. Then you simply restock the rack every two weeks and pick up your cash from the storeowner. Sounds easy. In reality, most of your products will be stolen by kids or the storeowner. The guy you made the deal with will cheat you or the whole rack will disappear. Another variation of this involves gumball machines, and that's just as risky.

Another straw is in futures trading. A complete course for $149.95. You will be rich in just five weeks. In day trading, a fortune can be made (or more likely, lost!) by using your home computer. Just imagine, no more suits and ties. You can work in your pajamas right in the den! This is probably the greatest risk you can take with your life savings. They say that day trading is just like casino gambling, except the food is better at the casino. You probably remember the case of the day trader who lost a fortune, killed his entire family, then went to the broker's office and killed some of the traders before taking his own life. Day trading can go wrong fast and it's not for the beginners.

Franchises—there are some great ones out there, but you will end up being the boss of a gang of 16-year-old burger-flippers or pizza-delivery guys if you are successful at qualifying for a major chain. There are also franchises that require large sums of cash that can be considered pie-in-the-sky deals. They don't have a track record, but the "idea" seems good. These are extremely risky and should be avoided.

When I suggest that you don't grab at straws, I do not mean that you should ignore suggestions or opportunities. I would investigate thoroughly every opportunity and get expert advice. I have done many bankruptcy appraisals in my career and every one could have been avoided if the owners

## The Straws

had invested in a $5 pocket calculator. If they would have sat down and analyzed the opportunity, they would not have been in trouble.

Let's say you are going to buy a restaurant. Add up all the expenses—rent, supplies, heat, electric bills, taxes, insurance, employees, maintenance, advertising, phone, accountants, attorney—and get the grand total for a month. Decide what your hours are for the month: 40, 50, or 60 per week, times four weeks. Take the number of hours per week and divide this into the monthly expenses and you will see what you have to net per hour to crack the nut! This is just the break-even figure. Add the profit factor and if you find that you must charge $21.75 for a hamburger, fries, and small cola, you know it cannot work!

Evaluate every opportunity thoroughly and don't get involved if your calculator tells you it's a no-no. A few years ago, I jumped into building a laundromat. After I started and

*You're Fired!*

the money was being sucked up by this project, I sat down with my calculator and did the math. Rent, tax, water, electric, equipment, etc, divided by hours per month at 24 hours per day. I was amazed at my conclusion. I carried it out further by figuring how many quarters were in a cubic foot. I then calculated the cubic feet in a 10-wheel dump truck. My discovery was it would take two dump trucks full of quarters each month to make money! Can you visualize two big trucks full of quarters instead of dirt?

   It's best to cut your losses as soon as you can. I decided to sell right away and I discovered that the owner of the pizza shop across from the laundromat did not have a $5 pocket calculator, so he was a good candidate for this deal. I sold him the business and I concentrated on other projects that my calculator told me had some chance of making money. Check out every deal before you grab at the straw.

# Contract Work

In the past, many people were loyal to the big giants of industry. I worked with old geezers who had never missed a day of work in 25 years! In those days, General Motors, Kodak, IBM, and Xerox rewarded loyalty by offering employment from cradle to grave. Many sons and daughters followed in their parent's footsteps.

Today those corporate giants don't give a rat's ass if you have perfect attendance for 20 years. They look at the bottom line—the stockholder always wins. They will draw a line through your name without any hesitation and you will be rewarded for your devotion by getting a free pass to the unemployment line. These big companies have learned that by discharging the loyal company workers for whom they have to pay ongoing expenses such as health insurance, payroll taxes, and unemployment insurance, they can keep their bottom line in order.

These loyal workers are then replaced by "contract" help. The contract personnel are paid a flat wage per hour and no benefits. They can be discharged with a simple "Get lost" and receive no severance pay, unemployment benefits, or two-week notices. If the job is finished, so are the contract workers. These workers are also called "jobbers."

I have worked with many jobbers over the years and they were some of the most interesting people I ever met. There is an old saying that there are only three reasons to become a jobber: 1) you have problems with alcohol, 2) you want to make a lot of money fast, or 3) you have an unhappy marriage (since most jobbers travel to the jobs, they are away from their families). In all the jobbers that I met, I never found one that did not fit one of those three categories. I might also add: 4) you are wanted by the police. I can remember a local policeman coming to the gate due to a minor traffic accident in the company parking lot and 90 percent of the jobbers hiding in the bathroom for the next hour!

A trick many of the jobbers used was to borrow an identity. If you were a certified Class A wire-puller on an atomic power project in North Dakota and had union or government identification, this could be duplicated and your brother-in-law's photo attached. He may actually have been a sweeper or maintenance man, but with his new identification he could go to New Jersey and work as a certified Class A wire-puller at the new atomic power plant for five times as much money! In my associations with jobbers I found this to be a fact many times.

Why am I telling you this information? Getting your foot in the door of a company is 90 percent of the battle of getting a job. My beautiful, intelligent, charming secretary did just that. Her husband was working as a salesman for our company and she accompanied him to the office frequently and

*Contract Work*

assisted him in making appointments. When our secretary of seven years did not show up one day, she offered her services. We found out she was twice as good as our old secretary and she is still here after two years!

Being a jobber will get your foot in the door. Once you have a chance to prove yourself to the company, you may have the opportunity to "go direct." You must do an excellent job at the contract position, and not appear to be of the same mold as the other contract people. While reason 2 of the description was "you want to make a lot of money fast," you must make it appear that your main interest is not the money. When you get your check each week, don't smile, drool, or jump up and down, and no somersaults. Just put it in your pocket and keep working.

If the company needs extra direct employees, they most certainly look at contract workers first. If you are looking for a direct job with the benefits, keep your nose clean. Do not hang with the jobbers during lunch or breaks. Try to associ-

ate with the direct employees. But you may find that you enjoy the vagabond lifestyle of being a contract worker. If this fits your plan, you may have your new career already. You can stop reading now!

The contract worker, when working away from home, sometimes receives a per-diem pay in addition to his wages. The per-diem money is used to defray expenses such as room and board and meals while away from home. This is known in the business as P.D. The first thing a jobber asks another jobber when he hears about a job is, "What's the P.D.?" Some people can live on the P.D. and bank (or drink) the wages. Those contract workers have several newsletters that list the job openings, the wages, the chance of overtime, and the P.D. If you are considering the contract-work profession, consult your library or the Internet to find these publications.

# The Volunteer

There is an old saying in the army: "Never volunteer for nuttin.'" A friend of mine, Laverne Thomas, told me many years ago, "Volunteers know exactly what their time is worth!" (Nothing!) These old sayings usually apply, but in this case, your goal is to infiltrate the company, see who the hiring honcho is and demonstrate your superior ability while he is passing by. Getting your foot in the door is your No. 1 goal. Remember the story about the Trojan horse? Being a volunteer will get you the same results—you get inside.

If you are a video technician, you may want to hit on one of the public TV channels. If you have expertise in communication, volunteer to do the school paper, town paper, union paper, or company paper. Do not volunteer for "dead-end" jobs because you will just be wasting time that you could

*You're Fired!*

spend looking for gainful employment. Getting on the inside will give you a chance to meet employers and employees, see the layout of the company, the working conditions, and the benefits available to the staff. Nearly every organization uses volunteers and it's easy to become one.

One tip: Don't volunteer 40 hours a week to any one organization. Tell them you can give them 10 hours depending on your schedule. This will enable you to volunteer with three or four other groups and get exposure to those groups as well. You can check out a lot of places using this method and the more exposure you get, the greater your chances of getting an offer of permanent employment.

*Never ever* let them know you are looking for work when you apply to volunteer. If they ask what you do, you can mumble something about research (after all, you *are* researching their joint) or working as a consultant (didn't your wife ask your advice on something this morning?). After you are there for a week or so and if you feel that this may be a good place to hang your hat, start the employment route by asking for an application or presenting your résumé.

If you need tax deductions, keep good records of your time, gas, and expenses, and consult with your accountant. I have known many people who used the volunteer procedure to latch onto a steady paycheck. Give it a try.

# The Consultant

As soon as your pink slip is in your pocket, stop at a local printer and have business cards made up. Toss your old business cards with your old company's name on them in the trash. Start handing out your new cards that say "consultant" on them.

A consultant is usually someone who has been fired from his job as advertising director, personnel director, or engineer, and since he has some exposure in those fields, he has become a consultant. (Obviously, he did not have enough skill or was bad at the job, otherwise he still would be there.) He is now available on an hourly basis to advise your company on how to get the phone to ring more, or your computer to do more per week by upgrading to the newest chip. A consultant does not need an office, staff, desk, secretary, computer, or any of the items usually considered necessary to start a business. All he needs is a business card and a phone or answering service. If someone falls for your consultant scheme, you will get the same opportunity that the contract worker or the volunteer got. You get your foot in the door! You must be very careful to not advertise your ignorance. Don't bite off more than you can chew.

If the job that you are consulting on is over your head, evaluate it carefully. Write an elaborate report on the amplitude of the project and, as a conclusion, indicate that they should hire a consultant who specializes in nuclear dental drills or such. You will gain a few hours of employment and arrive at an answer that keeps the boss happy. During this time, you have evaluated their cafeteria, their accommodations, how smart the bosses are, and if you would like to be one of the people on the staff.

Years ago I used this very ploy to become a "visualizer" for a large national corporation and it worked well. If this opportunity presents itself, you may find it interesting. I was tested many times by the direct employees because they were jealous that I was cutting into their meal ticket. They would ask to borrow certain items to test to see if I really had some experience in the field. One day I had several of the visualizer tools on my desk and another visualizer asked if he could borrow my "pig sticker." Since I had absolutely no idea what it looked like, I pretended to search over my desk to find one. After a few minutes of looking around and not saying anything, the guy reached over and picked up a small object with a pin sticking out of it. I said, "Oh, I knew it was here someplace." The guy gave me a strange look and walked away. I thought he was on to me, but a few weeks later, he asked me to go to a job in another city and help him for the weekend, so he must have decided that I had the ability (I didn't!). I did go with him and we did the job.

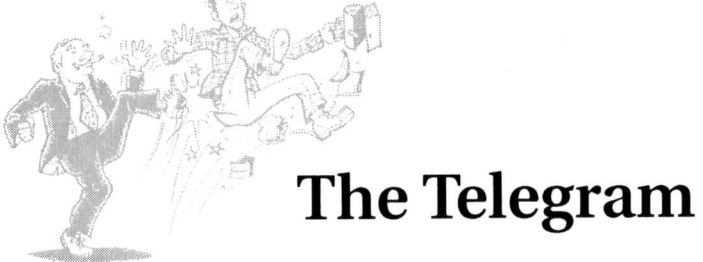

# The Telegram

Dot-dot-dash-dash-click-click. The word "telegram" brings back visions of the old telegraph operator clicking away at the hand-operated codes, sending an important message over the wire to a distant city. Has it been replaced by today's fiber optics, satellite receivers, e-mail and just plain cheap long distances? Maybe. The idea of this book is to give you some insight on how to find a job, and since you are competing for this job with hundreds of others, you need any help you can get. A telegram might be the little touch that makes your application get looked at!

Here are a couple of stories about telegrams. One you can possibly use, the other I just can't resist telling.

OK, here is one you may actually use. A guy shows up for an open interview and finds that 73 other applicants are

already there. Each one has been assigned a number and his is No. 74. He evaluates his odds and discovers that they will probably find a suitable candidate for the job long before his number comes up. He leaves the office with his number and heads for a phone. He calls Western Union and sends a telegram to the person conducting the interview. It reads "Urgent! Do not hire anyone until you see No. 74."

Guess what? No. 74 got the job. Ingenuity pays off.

Now, the other telegram (which has nothing to do with getting a job).

Being in the real estate business, over the years I have owned quite a few rental units. Quite a while ago, I had a rooming house. The inhabitants of this house were elderly people on fixed incomes. The rooms were sparsely furnished and, therefore, cheap to rent. An average room was 9x10, had a bare light bulb in the ceiling, a window with a dirty curtain overlooking the alley, a metal bed with a lumpy mattress, a

## The Telegram

chair, a dresser and that was it. They shared a bath with 10 other misfits.

I had one tenant, Bill, who was elderly and just had lost his part-time job, had no friends, and only one relative, his sister, Rose, who lived about 1,200 miles away.

Bill was certainly a lonely old coot; his only entertainment was a 9" black and white TV with rabbit ears and a fuzzy picture. Each and every Christmas, Easter, Thanksgiving, New Year, Fourth of July, Memorial Day, and, most anticipated of all, his birthday, Rose would send homemade cookies, a fruit cake, or a nice card with a sawbuck inside. Rose never missed an important date and Bill was at the mailbox each holiday waiting to hear from her. Since he had no phone, this was just about his only contact with his only sibling.

Finally, his birthday arrives and lo and behold, the mailman is empty-handed. Bill is depressed beyond belief. He sulks back to his desolate room. Rose had never forgotten him before.

About two hours later there is a knock at his door. Keep in mind that this is in the day and age of the "singing" telegram. When someone wanted to really impress someone else, they would send the singing telegram. A carrier from Western Union would arrive and sing "Happy Birthday," "Jingle Bells," or whatever was appropriate. Bill quickly answered the door and was greeted by a uniformed Western Union carrier. He said he had a telegram for Bill. Bill's spirits were immediately lifted and he gleefully said, "Sing it! Sing it!"

The carrier said, "I don't like to sing these things."

Bill excitedly implored, "Please sing it!"

The carrier said, "Oh, all right. Da, de, da, dum. Your sister, Rose, is dead."

# Hobbies

Everybody has some hobby. You may not realize you have a hobby, but nearly everyone has something they like to do with their free time. Now that you have a big chunk of free time, why not turn your hobby into an occupation? If your hobby is watching football or baseball on television, don't think it's impossible to make an occupation out of it. Have you ever watched a NASCAR race on Sunday? Did you notice the hundreds of different products that appear on the screen? Every driver's uniform, jacket, cap, race car, hauler, flag, banner, and trophy has a name on it! Don't you think the sponsors who pay $10 million a year would like to know exactly how many minutes or seconds their name is on the screen each week? There are companies who produce these calculations and there is nothing to stop you from starting one.

*You're Fired!*

Think over everything you like to do—fish, hunt, shop in the market or mall. These things can be converted into jobs. Many companies hire people to shop their stores to check out employees' friendliness or thievery. Theft is a big thing and building supply companies will sometimes hire people to buy a bunch of 2x4s and offer the kid loading it a few bucks to make the bunch bigger. If you like bicycles, model trains, or model planes, try opening a bike or hobby shop and make business a pleasure.

Do you work out? Like to sweat a little each day? Do they need instructors? Can you convert this hobby into a job? Give it a try.

You say you don't have any hobbies?

Do you stop off at the local topless tavern on your way home for a cocktail or two?

This is a hobby that could pay off big. You could become

a Realtor and specialize in selling these establishments. (I did and I have sold almost every boob joint in the city I live in at least once! It's a tough job, but somebody has to do it!) You could buy the place, become a D.J., bouncer, or bartender. Maybe even a dancer, depending on your sex. There are many employment opportunities under your nose, no matter what your hobby is.

A friend of mine liked to visit adult entertainment establishments and noticed that they were hard to find in the city. Regulations kept them out of the main areas and did not allow them to congregate in central locations. Most were on back alleys with little visibility. He had the idea of getting an ad from each juice joint and making up a booklet showing their locations as well as photos of the star attractions and their specials. In two short years, this little booklet has become a semi-monthly edition of 80 pages in color and covers three states! Not a bad job and it started from his hobby.

Make a list of your favorite things, hobbies, and places you go to have fun. Go over this list carefully and see if any of these things could be converted to a gainful occupation. You may surprise yourself.

# Training

Everyone has some skills. Even if your job was saying, "Do you want fries with that?" you have a skill. Since you are pounding the pavement now, the skills that you possess are evidently not in big demand. Since you have time to kill, training will make you more valuable *if* you train yourself for a job that is in demand.

I once had a friend whose son was laid off at a manufacturing plant. He suggested that his son join the military and get some training. I said that's a great idea—he can learn computers, welding, auto mechanics, or any number of useful trades. And when he gets out, there is a demand for his skills! For two years his father told me how good his son was doing in the service. When he was discharged, I talked with him and inquired what he had been training for. He proudly told me that after two years of intense training, he was now a gunner's mate, 1st class! I may be wrong, but I have never seen an ad in the employment section of the daily fish wrapper that anyone was hiring gunner's mates, 1st class! What a waste of time! Keep this in mind when you decide on what type of training you are looking for.

Many companies, unions, or even unemployment offices offer training or apprenticeships. Check out the opportunities carefully and be sure the task you are shooting for will not be easily replaced by some automation or become obsolete in a few years. Some training requires years of hard work (such as becoming an attorney, doctor, pilot, or engineer), but if you already possess one of these skills and have some

## Training

down time, you may want to add a specialty to your skill. Some skills are easily attainable with a minimum of time (real estate sales, auto mechanic, carpenter) and once you gain a little skill in these fields, you can earn a living while having the skills to produce a higher income.

Keep a look out for unusual professions that interest you. Sports require officials and if you have a particular interest in a sport, you may consider training in the rules and regulations for that sport with an eye toward being an official. As you walk around, keep your eyes open for jobs that appeal to you. They need not be 9-5 jobs, which restrict your ability to have fun. A bus driver for a tour company gets to travel to nice places, gets good pay, tips from the little blue-haired ladies, and meals while on the road. Training is easy. (Right pedal makes it go, left makes it stop, make sure the people are inside before pushing right pedal. Get the idea? )

Train yourself only for something that you can get bucks for and that will not give you an ulcer. There are hundreds of unusual jobs you may train for without committing to a four-year college.

# Sales Jobs

The most important person in the United States is not the president, the governor, the mayor or the owner of the largest factory. The most important person in the United States is the salesman! Sales is where it's at. Sales is where the money is. If there were not salesmen in the field, nothing could take place. Trucks would not be bringing items to the store if a salesperson did not sell the storeowner those items. GM could make the best cars in the world in the shortest period of time using the best materials, and if there were no car salesmen, there would be a big pile of cars at the end of the assembly line and that line would grind to a halt! Every item you use every day is there because of a salesman. Your medicine, your food, your clothing all gets to you as a result of salespeople.

*You're Fired!*

There are two types of salesmen. The first is a commissioned salesman. He gets a commission on what he sells. The more he sells, the more he makes, and I personally believe that this job is the best in the world. If you don't think that the salesman has the most important job in the universe, take a look at Xerox. A new CEO was hired and he decided to monkey around with the sales force. Salesmen who were familiar with certain products and customer's needs were transferred to different areas. New salesmen were assigned and in a few short months, the sales plummeted. The stock, which had been up near $100 a share, dove to less than $5. Obviously, the CEO got the ax, but the damage was already done. Salesmen make the world go around.

The other type of salesman is paid by the hour or week, no matter what he sells or how much. The incentive is not there and I really consider these geeks to be "order takers" rather than real salespeople. This position usually attracts lazy people.

What does it take to be a commissioned salesperson? Do you need to have good clothes, a nice car, great sales ability, a superb personality, and ambition? All that does not hurt, but the most important item in any salesperson's bag of tricks is "knowledge of the product." If you know everything about the product—all the good things and especially all the bad things—you will be in demand. The other qualities are nice, but knowledge is the main item.

You have heard it said that a sharp salesman could sell refrigerators to Eskimos (yes, Eskimos *do* buy refrigerators). I have never been able to sell someone something he did not want (and I have tried), but if someone *wants* something, you probably could not stop him from buying it. If you can explain what you are selling so that a layperson can understand it and it's something he needs, your job is done.

There are hundreds of books, audiotapes, videos, and seminars that can teach you sales technology, and they are all good.

*Sales Jobs*

Selling a vacuum cleaner uses the same principals as selling a luxury car or house. If you decide to try selling, go for the big-ticket items. I have always wondered why someone rings my doorbell and spends half an hour trying to sell me some cheap item like a magazine subscription or some revolutionary new soap powder. If he is successful, he will have made $3.55. I know many car salesmen who could write a car deal in the same time and make some real money, not just $3.55.

The car salesman is one of the most important people in America. If that salesman does not sell you a nice, shiny new car, our economy can be seriously affected. Detroit does not build cars if they are not sold, and when Detroit does not build cars, the suppliers of steel, tires, glass, plastic, paint, and accessories feel the pinch. The chain reaction is felt in every city and state.

This guy in the plaid suit with the cowboy hat and cigar standing in the car lot of your local dealership can do more to

help our economy than the president and all the brokers on Wall Street. He is a commissioned salesperson, and by putting you behind the wheel of your dream car, he makes a good buck. His hours are flexible, and he may sell as many cars on the golf course as he sells on the car lot.

Some people view the car-sales professionals as a lowly lot due to past dealings with car salesmen, but I believe it is an excellent job opportunity. I have met many salesmen who not only made a lot of money, but actually purchased the dealership where they were employed. The educational requirements are not severe. You should have knowledge of automobiles and financing. You will meet a lot of people, and if you are successful, you will make a lot of money. I'm not saying that everybody who is unemployed should head for the nearest auto store, but I'm just using this profession because everybody has dealt with a car salesman at one time or another. Think back . . . how long did it take for you to buy your jalopy? A half-hour, 45 minutes tops probably, and the salesman pocketed some nice change.

Every item in our lives has to be sold by a salesman. Look over the sales opportunities in your local paper and consider this job. Remember, all it takes is knowledge of the product and a little ambition.

# The Phonies

As I mentioned in the chapter on grabbing at straws, there are businesses that cater to the unemployed. They are looking for your grocery money. I'm going to give you a tip on how to analyze the pitch. I have written hundreds (maybe thousands) of ads and every one is designed to bring the good to your attention and distract you from seeing the bad. Check out the ad on the next page.

Let me point out all the good that this ad emphasizes:

- *At home.* Home is a nice word. Visualize the fireplace, the cat curled up in your lap, and the smell of a pot roast cooking in the oven.
- *No previous experience needed.* Anybody can do this job! This does not even rule out illiterate morons. (Except that

they couldn't read the ad to apply!)
- *No commuting.* You don't even need a car, gas, or bicycle.
- *No selling.* Everybody dislikes selling for fear of rejection.
- *Work the hours you choose.* Spend all day at the gin mill and just hit the keyboard when you get home all liquored-up.
- *Greatest job opportunity of your life.* I'm sure!
- *If you can type or are willing to learn.* About 75 percent of the people in the United States can type. Some with only two fingers, but the ad says "willing to learn," so they must be planning on teaching you.
- *Our experts.* You will be trained by experts at signing you up for this profession.
- *Free facts at the seminar.* I'll bet you will also get coffee and a doughnut!
- I almost left out the *up to $35,000 a year!* I guarantee that they can show you a bunch of checks payable to Mary Smith, transcriptionist from Dr. I. Sawbones, M.D. that total 35 grand.

Now, let's go back and read between the lines.

The seminar will show you how easy it is to use your keyboard and their software ($595.95) to create medical histories on a CD/ROM. If you can't type, they will sell you the video

## The Phonies

*Typing for Idiots* ($29.95). Let's just consider this: How does the good doctor do these histories right now? Are they kept forever on cassettes? Does he have the bimbo at the receptionist's desk do them in her free time? Are doctors not eligible to buy the same software that these guys are trying to sell you? Do you think the good doctor wants to free up his receptionist's time so she can do her nails more often? Are not medical records confidential records? Does he want you to take them home and maybe even lose them since he has no idea who you are or if you are trustworthy?

Let's take the great "no commuting" feature of this ad. Combine it with the "no selling" feature. Has a doctor ever called you and asked you to transcribe his patient files? I don't think so. This means you will have to advertise in a medical publication (which will cost around $200) and hope a doctor who has no one transcribing his files calls you on your ad. When no calls come in on your ad, you might call the doctor and make an appointment to see him regarding transcribing his medical files. Have you ever had a fever of 110 degrees, throwing up your cookies, and called your doctor for an emergency appointment, and he says, "I can fit you in two weeks from Tuesday at 5 P.M."? Now you are calling strange doctors and asking for a *sales* appointment! Good luck!

So finally you do get an appointment with Dr. Death and you arrive at the appointed hour. You now have involved "commuting" and you are going to attempt to "sell" your service to the doc (after an hour's wait with all the coughing, wheezing patients). So your luck is with you and he tells you that for the past 11 years he has been piling up audio cassettes and the job is yours for $2.25 per tape, and all you need is a rental truck to pick them up and take them home! Or he tells you that he presently has a transcription service that puts them on CD/ROMs for $2.25 per tape and he will be glad to switch to you if you can beat that price, say about $1.99 per tape! Are you discouraged, yet? Did I mention that you certainly need a computer ($1,000) and access to the Internet (about $200 per year)?

Don't worry. At the rear of the room where the free seminar is held, there will be several tables and pitch men ready to supply you with everything you need to get started (yes, they take MasterCard/Visa). The only thing they cannot supply is the clients for your new business.

Evaluate every ad as I have this one and you will not be chasing rainbows that end in a pot of crap instead of a pot of gold.

# Becoming an Entrepreneur

There is an old saying in the engineering field: "Six months ago, I didn't even know how to spell engineer and now I *is* one!" I can almost transpose that saying to my own circumstances: "A few years ago, I didn't even know how to spell entrepreneur and now I is one!"

Until I decided to start my own business, my ratio of firings to hirings was exactly the same! I decided to change that situation by becoming my own boss. I *like* me, so there is very little chance I would *fire* me. Being my own boss was the solution. One thing you discover as soon as you become your own boss is that you aren't. Every customer is your boss. You go from one boss to hundreds of bosses, so get used to it. Keep in mind that if one of those hundreds of bosses fire you, you still have a job, you just don't work for that boss again.

## You're Fired!

As I mentioned previously, Xerox fired lots of people over the years (that's right, I wasn't the only one!) and I'm sure they canned these people because they were worthless to the company. About the same time, I "retired" from the big X, an Indian gentleman also hit the bricks. He was well educated, and since his services to the company were in the communication field, he decided to give owning a telecommunication business a try. He started out selling phone equipment to small businesses and today he is president of one of the largest telecommunication companies in the area (he is on page 110 of the directory of Xerox "has beens" that I mentioned).

Being fired actually opens the door to greater opportunities. This gentleman, in a recent article, tells how he felt useless and discouraged upon being let go. Becoming an entrepreneur who controlled his own life was the best thing that ever happened to him.

If you start your own business, you will find that "your own hours" will turn into "long, long hours," but you won't mind because that's going to produce results. If you are not afraid of long hours, do go into your own business. When I retired two years ago, I told my wife that I was going to cut back on the hours I worked each week. I followed through on that promise and I cut back to 40-45 hours a week!

In addition to long hours, be prepared for very little income, unless of course you have a lot of money to start or buy an existing established business. When I started, I did not buy an existing business and I had very little money. Very, very little money. It was not uncommon for the power company to pull my plug or the phone company to cut my lines. I actually became so acquainted with the shut-off crew from the power company that I sold two of them houses and one of their children rented an apartment from me (reinforcing my theory that everything happens for the better).

The first secretary that I employed asked me at the end of

*Becoming an Entrepreneur*

the second week when payday was. I said, "I dunno." I can still remember the look on her face! Then I asked her if I could borrow $10 and she let me take it! She stayed about two years and married the son of one of our salesmen. Starting out can mean some lean times, but you should expect it. At one time, I actually qualified for food stamps!

If you decide to go the self-employed trail, be sure to get an accountant familiar with small businesses and an attorney you can work with. It's best to pick ones that are approximately your age or younger. The reason is if you use your father's attorney, who is older, you will have to change in the future when he or she dies or retires. Changing attorneys or accountants can be a disaster. You will also need a good insurance carrier to protect your ass and assets in case something goes wrong.

Becoming an entrepreneur is easy. There are just two

*You're Fired!*

ways to start. You buy an existing business or you start a new one from scratch like I did. What determines the method? You have a lot of money, you buy an existing business. You have pocket change (and a lot of guts), you start from scratch.

Let's take buying a business, first. What would you pay me for a list of possible businesses that could be for sale? $50? $100? If you mail me (Andy Kane, 1942 E. Main St., Rochester, NY 14609) a check for just $25, I will give you this information immediately and for your geographical area.

OK, stop reading, write the check, and get it in the mail right now. Don't read any further until you come back from the mailbox. Pause, pause, pause . . . Did you get that check in the mail? All right, read on.

Do you have a coffee table or a phone stand with your phone on it? Good. Walk over and pick up your local Yellow Pages. In here, you will find a list, by classification, of every business in your geographical area that could be for sale. Pick out a business heading that you like and start contacting the owners, or use the shotgun approach and have a form letter printed:

---

Business owner,

I am interested in purchasing an office-cleaning business. I would retain your present staff, if possible. If you are not interested in selling at this time and you know of another office-cleaning business that may be for sale, please contact me at 555-1234.

Thank you.

—Mr. I. Clean Jr.

Keep it simple. Don't mention you have lots of cash. Do mention that you would keep their staff, because many owners don't want to be the ones that use the magic words, "You're fired." The letter says you'll keep the present staff, "if possible." After you take over, you can dismiss any that you don't like!

Almost every business type has a "clearing house" or organization that oversees or assists that type of business. It may be a union or trade association. These are excellent places to find out who is retiring or selling a business.

If you have time (I'm sure you do!), you can call businesses. Ask for the owner or manager and inquire if they may be selling now or in the near future. Always ask if they know of any businesses that may be for sale. This gets you double the results of one call.

Business brokers are an ideal place to look. Lots of Realtors devote full time to selling the ivy-covered cottages with the white picket fences to newlyweds, but some specialize in selling businesses (I do!) and they have the knowledge and experience to set you on the right track.

As in any dealings, remember "Buyer Beware." Many business owners kite the income and eliminate some of the expenses in the final years so that the business looks good on paper. I once had a trailer court for sale. There were about 100 trailer sites and a general store on the property. The trailer court owner also operated the general store. The entire package was reasonably priced based on the site rentals, but the individual site rentals seemed about $100 higher per month than the other trailer parks in the area. The buyer and I decided to investigate further and we picked a few units, knocked on the doors and asked what the rental for the site was. All verified the rents that were indicated on the profit and loss statement. The buyer completed the transaction and took title to the property. He also became the owner of the general store where the tenants paid their site fee each month. When the following month came around, the new owner gleefully awaited the tenants. The first one came in and paid the stated amount (that you remember was about $100 higher than neighboring trailer courts). The owner gave the tenant his receipt and the tenant just stood there waiting. The new owner asked what he was waiting for. The tenant said, "My chips!" Further discussion revealed that the owner had given each tenant back $100 in plastic chips that could be used in his store for pop, beer, and other store items.

It's like the old trick of salting the mine. A mine owner who was trying to sell a played-out mine would load a shotgun with gold dust and fire it into the walls of the mine. A prospective buyer would believe that there was still gold in them thar hills and buy the mine!

Check out every opportunity carefully. There are ways to check every type of business other than looking at the books. A buyer of a beer joint can sneak around and count the empty bottles or cans on trash day. Check with suppliers who deliver to a business and see if the deliveries match the books. Buying an existing business is good if you can determine that the mine has not been salted!

Now, let's get down to starting a business from scratch.

What would you pay me for a list of possible businesses that you could start? $50? $100? If you mail me (Andy Kane, 1942 E. Main St., Rochester, NY 14609) a check for just $19.95 (discount for previous customers!), I will give you this information immediately and for your geographical area.

You guessed it, didn't you? Grab that phone book again and thumb through until you hit on something that tickles you. Keep in mind the level of your education and the start-up funds you have accumulated from your last two unemployment checks. Obviously, you have to start small and it will probably be a one-person show (you) to start. If you have a wife or girlfriend, they may be useful for office duty (if you have a wife *and* girlfriend, I suggest having them work alter-

*Becoming an Entrepreneur*

nate days!). Kids that can walk and talk? I used all this cheap labor to start.

If the business you choose requires licensing or education, take that into consideration and be sure to obtain all the necessary documents before you start. Starting a business is hard, but it's even harder if you are starting while in the Gray Bar Hotel! Keep it legal. No book or manual can possibly tell you everything you need to get started in a new business, but there are many sources to guide you depending on what field you choose. Nearly every occupation has an association that governs or assists its members. Find the one for your chosen business and join or subscribe. The names of these organizations can be found on the Internet or in your library.

I believe the library can beat the Web for research on many business topics. The Web's convenience should be balanced against the amount of time needed to do a thorough search for information. Libraries can be much better when you want printed directories and other materials, such as state and city demographics; training assistance; meeting rooms for quiet research or talks with clients; or teleconferencing facilities for virtual meetings and distance learning.

When you own your own business, you also become your own advertising department, and the disbursement of your advertising dollars must be carefully planned.

I have a friend who worked in a sewer treatment plant (I'll call him "Norton") and during the Super Bowl, he could tell immediately when a commercial interrupted the game by the sudden rush in the sewer pipes! Super Bowl commercials cost more per minute than any other television advertising, but since most who watch the game are die-hard football geeks who do not want to miss one second of the game, the commercials are bathroom breaks.

If someone does not see or hear your 15-second spot on TV or radio, it's gone forever. The print media is a better buy. An ad in a local flyer hangs around until the garbage is wrapped in it and even then, the garbage man may read it and call you. An ad in the Yellow Pages is an excellent investment. You don't need a huge ad, just a small one will do. The ad for my rental business is just a one-liner, in bold type to stand out. It's not expensive. It's in the book for a year or so and usually the phone company just adds it to your bill each month, so you don't need the year's costs up front!

>Alhepa Apts. 500 Alhepa Cir . . . . . . . . . . . . . .555-0036
>Alspaz Companies 5353 Buffalo Rd . . . . . . . .555-6300
>**ALLSTATE RENTALS**
>  **1941 E. Main** . . . . . . . . . . . . . . . . . . . . . . . .**482-7946**
>Ambassador Apts. 68 S. Union . . . . . . . . . . .555-7624
>Anzalak Properties 7514 East Ave . . . . . . . . .555-5057

This ad produces hundreds of calls weekly. As you grow, you can add other types of ads. I suggest advertising on products that hang around homes or businesses, such as calendars. These will keep your name in front of the public for extended periods of time.

Billboard locations must be carefully chosen. A low-rent location may be cheap, but business will suck unless you are selling booze, guns, or knives. Your business should have a prominent address (like Main Street!) if you depend on being found by customers. Buy the location if you can to avoid rental fees that do not build up equity. If you buy, try to buy a multi-use building so that your office location is subsidized by rent from other tenants in the building.

Give entrepreneurship a try. The worst that can happen is you are back collecting unemployment insurance.

# Some Tips

One important thing to consider when buying or starting a business is safety. Remember the old saying, "The three most important factors in real estate are: location, location, location"? Unless you are well armored or like violence, stay in a safe neighborhood. One big attraction of the cash-and-carry stores in every bad neighborhood is the huge amount of cash they take in. Their books will look good even if half the cash is skimmed off! But these big piles of cash don't just attract business buyers, they also attract robbers, crack heads and other types that don't mind firing a few shots to get your attention. Some of those shots may end your entrepreneurship and your regular breathing! Safety first!

Another thing that must be considered if you are buying an established business is having a "covenant not to compete." Many people will sell a business that has been around for 25 years and has an established clientele. Next week, they open a similar business a block away and all your customers are gone. It can happen. Even if the seller of the business is 90 years old and speaking of retiring to Miami Beach, ask for a covenant not to compete.

For example, did you ever hear of Ryder truck rental? When James A. Ryder sold the company, the buyer assumed that Mr. Ryder was headed to the rocking chair and so did not arrange a covenant not to compete in the contract. A few weeks later, a new truck rental company opens up. The name of this company is "Jartran," as in James A. Ryder Transportation! Put a "do not compete" clause in *any* offer to buy a business.

# Job Fairs

Many cities, convention bureaus, schools or even major employers sponsor job fairs or career expos. Many businesses set up booths to expose their company to the unemployed or underemployed. Usually the entire spectrum of jobs are available at one of these events.

A recent job fair I attended had management, sales, administration, insurance, manufacturing, marketing, finance, banking, retail, customer service, collections, restaurant/hotel management, hospitality, clerical, maintenance, telemarketing, health care, human resources, administrative, industrial, engineering, computer science, information systems, telecommunications, documentation, tech writing/editing, electro-mechanical technicians, Web developers, help-desk support, software developers, software

engineers, hardware engineers, test engineers, Windows developers, network support, database design, Lotus notes developer, network designs—all available under one roof!

You save lots of time and get personal contact with interviewers. Bring an armful of résumés. Keep them separated by different occupations, as you have designed them ahead of time. Don't be afraid to apply for a job outside your field. A friend of mine had a degree in engineering and once when that field was slow, he attended barber school. Now when the demand for engineers is dormant, he lays his slide rule down and grabs the scissors. (Depending on the head count, he says he makes almost the same hourly rate and has less pressure!) Picking up a second profession is a very good idea.

The job fair is also a good place to do some networking. Many of the attendees can brief you on their last employer. Just because they got the ax in manufacturing does not mean

## Job Fairs

the company is going down the road to no existence. They may be hiring in the engineering dept. Talk to everyone at the job fair, not just the human resource geeks! It's a great opportunity for exposure. Dress appropriately because you will be making a lot of first impressions today. If you normally wear a ring through some portion of your face, it's a good time to leave it home.

# Cyberjobs

Many companies post their job openings on the Web and this is good. You can see what they are looking for and tailor your résumé to those qualifications. The one thing that I do not like about this procedure is that it eliminates the face-to-face encounter and the personal contact that is probably the most important ingredient in getting the job. Most cyberopenings are for a warm body to sit in a cubicle. If you want to be a cubicle dweller, this is an excellent way to get your very own cubicle. If you are cube-shaped, drive a cubemobile and have a cube wife and two small cubes running around the house, you will be forever happy in a position like this.

Since you are without a job, this may be the right time to upgrade your employment to something that you like. I

*You're Fired!*

would suggest reviewing all the openings posted on the Web and then after responding via the Internet, making a personal visit to their human resources office. This will give you the best of both worlds and also show the company that you are more interested than the applicant who chooses to sit at his PC in his pajamas and fire off a response online. Of course, if the employer is 500 miles away, your response is limited to the electronic method.

# The Application

No matter what methods you use to contact employers—by mail, in person, or via the Internet—at some time you will have to fill out an application. This piece of paper is one of the most important documents in the entire employment process. It will actually *represent you* when you are not around. If you fill it out with a crayon, drool on it, spill a drink on it, or write illegibly, that will be the impression this document will give to the prospective employer. I'm sure you don't want an impression of being a moron transmitted to the interviewer in the human resources department.

I would make an application a work of art. Do not use cursive writing; carefully print every fact asked for on the application. Do not leave anything off the application. Anything left off may indicate to the person looking at the application that there is a problem. A missing Social Security number may indicate you are here illegally. A missing phone number may indicate that you are hiding from creditors. A missing beneficiary or emergency contact name when you have indicated that you're married may indicate marital problems. A post-office box number instead of a street address may imply that you're hiding from someone (either marshals or ex-wives) or are just plain shunning responsibilities. If you use a box number regularly, ask a friend if you can use his street address.

You may fill out many applications in your hunt for the perfect job, but each one is just as important as the last. If you take the time to visit the human services department, take the time to completely and legibly fill out the application. Although your résumé has most of the information that the application calls for, every employer wants it on his form and signed by you. If you don't have the time or the skill to sit right down and fill it out, take it home and do a good job printing or typing it in full. Be sure all addresses have zip codes and phone numbers have area codes. Even if they need your kind of help, chances are they will not spend hours trying to contact you. If they cannot reach you by phone, e-mail, or snail mail, they will simply go to the next application.

Be sure that any phone number you list has a competent person to answer it—no little kids or jokers. If the phone is attended by an answering machine, be sure the message is clear and short; no background music or funny voices. You want future employers to think you are serious. (At least until they hire you!)

I mentioned filling out everything on the application. If one of your last assignments was to design an explosion-proof light switch and the test blew the building up, I would extend the time at the previous job to cover the time spent at the now vacant lot.

Another no-no is relatives who work for the employer. Do

## The Application

not list your father who works in the shipping department. Many companies have policies against hiring relatives of employees. If, after you get hired, the boss says "Your name is Igor Plotzkie *Jr.*? Are you any relation to the Igor Plotzkie *Sr.* who works in shipping?" Act surprised and say, "That's my father! I've always wondered where he worked!" Since firing you would make them look like idiots for hiring you in the first place, they probably will ignore their family policy.

Applications are like time bombs—you never know when they are going to go off. If, after you get hired, another company calls you, check it out. I did and the second job paid a lot better than the first. I immediately packed up and headed for the second job!

# Face to Face

Here comes the terrifying part of the job search. Your hard work—applications, e-mails, résumés, and networking—has finally produced a face-to-face interview. This is the scary part, and don't tell me you aren't scared. It's a performance, and just like any rock star, comedian, or actor, before you walk on stage you are terrified.

When I was driving race cars and I was sitting on the racetrack with the engine shut off listening to *The Star Spangled Banner* play, I was a basket case. My heart was pounding and my blood pressure was sky-high. But as soon as the race started and I was in a pack of cars inches apart going 150 miles an hour, I was calm!

Everyone is nervous before a performance of any type. There is nothing you can do about it except realize that as soon as the interview begins, you will calm down.

Your résumé did its job and landed you an interview. The old Boy Scout motto comes into play here. Be prepared! You have three days to prepare, but are not sure where to begin. Nervousness sets in and you begin to wish the day would hurry up and arrive. It is easy to feel like your fate is in the hands of the interviewer and you are waiting for the "verdict."

Don't leave the success of your interview to chance! By using your time wisely and being proactive in your preparations, the impression you make on the employer will be much better.

Here are some suggestions to help you prepare and approach your interview with confidence:

*Be prepared emotionally when interview day arrives!* You are going in well prepared. Breathe deeply and let go of doubt and anxiety. Envision yourself shaking the hand of your new employer. Think positively about your ability to get the job and opportunities that lie ahead. Positive mental attitude is a must!

No matter how prepared you are, some things happen beyond our control. What if the job turns out to be vastly different that you expected? What if you don't "click" with the interviewer? How we react to these surprises is important. Remain upbeat and remember that opportunity may still come from the situation. Always put forth your best effort!

*Be healthy and rested.* The interviewer will notice if you have a low energy level due to lack of sleep or illness. Be sure to stay off the booze and get plenty of sleep in the days before your interview to enhance your ability to answer questions and think on your feet. If you have trouble falling asleep, a warm bath may calm you. Productively preparing for your interview instead of worrying will also help you sleep better! Try and get an interview in the morning if possible. The interviewer will not have had any bad experiences that day if you are the first one he sees and you will have arrived rested.

*Be punctual.* Be sure you know exactly where and when the interview will take place. If you are unfamiliar with the area or building, do a "test run" to make sure you allot enough time on the actual day, or prepare by looking at a map and giving yourself plenty of extra time. Arrive early so you can gain your composure instead of rushing into the interview. Note where the best parking is and be sure to have change if it is metered. You don't want to be worrying about your jalopy being towed during your interview.

*Research the company and industry.* There is no better way to impress a future employer than by having current and accurate information about the company, industry, and even the interviewer's background. Having this edge will help you replace feelings of helplessness or intimidation with enthusiasm (as you begin to picture yourself as part of the team) and confidence (as you realize you can converse intelligently with the interviewer).

Find information through publications such as annual reports, journals, press releases, trade magazines and people you know who work there. Facts to know about the company include:

- Products and services
- Competition
- Trends in the industry
- Number of employees
- Business locations
- Current challenges
- Marketshare or position in the market

I once went to an interview with a defense contractor. Information about this operation was scarce due to it being classified, but as I was waiting in the lobby I thumbed through some aerospace magazine and noticed they called missiles "birds." I also noticed that "thrust" was an important item when discussing the birds. As the interview began, the person conducting the interview mentioned that if I were hired, I would be working on a ground-to-air-missile. I asked, "What is the thrust of this bird?" I was immediately hired. It was a good thing I had thumbed through that magazine!

Another thing that will help considerably is bonding with the guy who is doing the interview. The interviewer no doubt has many outside interests. He may like to ski, sky dive, canoe, mountain climb, or take part in any number of activities. Look around the room. Are there any baseballs autographed by Sammy Sosa? Pictures of Dale Ernhardt on the wall? Bronzed ice skates? Try to figure out what his hobby is. I have actually been hired because the interviewer and I had a lot in common. They say it's not what you know, it's who you know and by becoming friendly with the interviewer, I was in!

*Rehearse for the part.* Try to anticipate the types of questions most likely to be asked in the interview such as: "Why should the company hire you?" Review your résumé and look for facts the interviewer may want more information about such as gaps in employment history or technical expertise.

Ask a friend or family member to "interview" you and provide constructive criticism regarding your presentational skills. During the interview did you touch your face repeatedly, squirm in your chair, talk too fast, or crack your knuckles? Keep in mind the more you practice being interviewed, the more confident you will be during actual interview situations. In fact, it is a good idea to accept all interview opportunities that come your way merely to practice. (You also never know what useful information you may discover during an interview, which may lead to another opportunity.) Do you have a video camera? Do your entire pitch into the camera and play it back to see how you come off.

*Dress neat and be clean.* This includes well-kept fingernails and hair. Do not use strong aftershave or perfume. If they are allergic to certain smells, many interviewers will cut short the interview just to get your smelly ass out of there. Do not overdress; no gold chains, Rolex watches, or big diamond rings when trying out for ordinary jobs. If you are going to an interview with a brokerage firm, the Rolex and silk suit may impress them, but you must tailor your appearance to fit the position you are interviewing for.

*Bring supporting materials.* Bring several résumés even though the interviewer probably has a copy. You never know if they have misplaced it or if they need to pass your résumé on to additional people. If you have a portfolio of work, bring it to the interview along with letters of reference and other evidence of your accomplishments such as awards and letters of recognition. Carry your materials in an attractive, professional case in order to make a positive impression and to demonstrate that you are organized and prepared.

Ask questions, but not too many. You should keep eye contact at all times with the interviewer. Don't ever mention politics, religion, or anything that may disturb the interviewer.

Keep in mind that although this interview is important, if you do not get the job, you will be no worse off than you were before the interview. Do your best and I wish you success.

# Wowee! Whoopee!

You got a bite! The phone rang or the mailman delivered an offer! Finally! There is a God!

What should you do when you receive the offer? Relax, think it over, and tell them you will let them know first thing tomorrow. Are the benefits what you expected? Equal or better than your last job? If overtime is worked, do you get paid for it? How many weeks of vacation? Are there stock options? Profit sharing? Union dues? Make a checklist and go over it carefully. Is the pay equal to other similar jobs in the area? Is there any chance for advancement? I once worked at a place where the advancement was directly related to who died or retired in the progression ahead of me.

The decision is yours. Do you need three weeks vacation when you have been off for six weeks now? Can you live on

*You're Fired!*

$30 less per week until they see how good you are? Many times the first offer a company makes is a test to see how cheaply you can be had. If you feel it is a test, tell them everything is great except the salary and you would jump at the job if it were 5 percent higher.

Be sure to call with your answer as agreed, so even if you don't get this particular job, they will not consider you irresponsible. It's never good to burn bridges. I once worked for the same company three different times in about five years and they probably would take me back again!

I hope you enjoy your new job and when you get your first paycheck, carefully fold a couple of twenties, place them in an envelope and mail them to . . . You know the address!

# What Do I Do With This Book Now?

You may, now that you have your wonderful job, decide to present this book to a friend who has recently lost his livelihood. Do not do that! Authors receive royalties only on books purchased, not given away. You may get the idea that I am greedy (true), but I am only looking out for you.

Do you remember in the beginning of this book that I mentioned that I had a talent for getting fired? Do you see those same characteristics in you? I do. You were fired before and you will be again. Keep this book with your family heirlooms and other valuable items. You *will* need it again.